The Definite Purpose

My definite purpose for this book is to inspire the subconscious mind of every reader to become more successful. This

1

book is a commitment. If you have made it this far then the commitment is already in play. Allow me to guide you.

Cycle 1

Thinking

The mind is everything. Therefore, everything is the mind. There is not one thing that exists that did not begin with one thought. Every thought is truly an invested process. Is your invested process bringing you the return of investment that you desire? If not, then perhaps it is 100% of what and how you are thinking. Join me in the first set of the seven *Keys for Thinking*.

3

The 1ˢᵗ Key Law

Keep Intuition Above Perception

Most human perception is based 100% on memory. You may have a perfect plan spot on for success, but memory can be the blockage from ever seeing it through. It could come from failing, family members unintentionally or intentionally, and even from television. Using you intuition as power over your perception can take you a very long way in one day, let alone a complete lifestyle. It is quite like the old-time fighting movies when the master always says "the answers are within" or whatever to the student. All the masters are saying is to keep intuition above

perception. Easier said than done I know; this is The First Key Law.

The 2ⁿᵈ Key Law

Always know what's next but remain in the present moment.

Daydreaming is a form of meditation. However, drifting off for too long would make remaining in the present moment quite a task to say the least. The *NOW is* where we are at our peak of power. In this very moment you are in 100% control. Drifting off too long is stripping the strength right out of you. Video games, social media, chit-chat, gossip, daydreaming about irrelevance, etc. are some of the most distracting things most people do with their time.

You can join social media groups that are tapped into the same frequency that you are going. You can gossip and daydream about where you are going as well. Always knowing what is next must not interfere with this very present moment that we breathe in every second.

The 3rd Key Law

Always ask why before asking how.

When you wonder "how" in a situation it raises doubtful thoughts. Doubt can be detrimental to one's plan if it raises too highly. On the contrary, seeking why before how raises a natural definite purpose. Nothing is manifested without it being a definite decision. Asking or wondering why it is necessary is a very powerful tool to raise and inspire your definite decision.

The 4ᵗʰ Key Law

Schedule 30 min a day just to think bigger than usual thoughts.

Visualization is a strong method used in manifesting your desires. Thinking bigger than normal thoughts brings that "kid" mentality back that most adults have lost over time. Children have very strong desires. As we all grow into adults, we are taught that "reality" isn't childish wishing so then we stop. I believe that both are needed. The "reality" as well as the big desires far from our present reach. Let us all

utilize this Forth Key Law as we tap back into our inner child.

The 5th Key Law

Doubt is a sin.

Confidence in a definite decision is the only way that the definite decision will work. When in doubt we create a mental blockage which ultimately defeats the purpose for a definite decision. Doubt is sprung mostly from memory stored in the subconscious mind. In most cases this is from early childhood when we hear things like "we aren't rich" or "that's impossible" from our family. This is very difficult to overcome but it is worth the work. Affirmations help a lot with rebranding your subconscious mind to the new successful thinking that we all desire.

The 6th Key Law

Identify wants vs. needs in every situation.

If you read my "Watch Me Work, Book One" then you remember me going over the want to need versus the need to want. This is simply a thought process instilled in every human. However, some are heavier on one side, as others are consistently balanced. The need to want can keep us from reaching our true potential. On the other hand, the want to need mentality can keep us from having fun and enjoying life. The perfect blended balance of the two can lead us to the perfect world that we all desire.

The 7th Key Law

Believe in yourself.

Only you and your thoughts can get you to your desired destination. Just as only you and your thoughts have guided you here to this book, and into your current life's situation. Believing in yourself is the solution to all your problems. Think positive and get out of your way. You have places to go.

Cycle 2

Realism

Accuracy when talking, honesty to self, and accepting the truth are ways of showing true realism. To become a realist is simply being realistic (not doubtful) in every situation that you encounter in life. The old saying "the truth shall set you free" means nothing to a realist, as he or she has been free for as long as they've been realists.

The 8th Key Law

a definite purpose + a definite goal = a definite decision.

Nothing has ever been accomplished without a definite decision of somewhat. In order to arrive at every definite decision ever made by mankind, there had to have been a definite goal with a definite purpose.

The 9th Key Law

Realize what's working vs. what's not.

It may sometimes be difficult to realize that a particular venture is just not working out. This is where a mastermind alliance really come in handy. Having different perspectives (partners) is very useful when the realization aspect is in motion. Shutting down a failure is not the same as quitting. It is a learning opportunity and a way to recover from losses. You cannot learn or recover much from quitting.

The 10th Key Law

Only invest in thoughts with a return of interest.

Thinking is powerful. However, realizing how you are thinking is even more powerful. The tenth key law defines terms like, "think positive" or "everything is good" in a clearer way. Every thought is an investment. What's your greatest mental investment?

The 11ᵗʰ Key Law

Know when it is time to listen only.

Have you ever heard that less is more? This is a fact when the eleventh key law is applied. Listening is the most informational tool that we have. The art of listening is an acquired skill that takes time to learn thoroughly. Reading is also a form of listening. Sometimes a person or business partner just needs to be heard with nothing else. Know how to be that.

The 12ᵗʰ Key Law

Always tell the truth.

The truth is the purest form of communication. Integrity is pretty much your DNA in the business world. If your reputation is respected for your integrity, you must always remain true to self. It's far more simpler than it sounds. Just tell the truth no matter what.

The 13ᵗʰ Key Law

Tune out the noise.

If it is not 100% something pertaining to your own life, then indeed it is noise. Television, gossip, radio, and even listening to your significant other's highly detailed story about their day can all be forms of noise. You can in fact be the same noise to your significant other as well. Tuning out the noise is putting more of a tunnel vision on your plan to succeed.

20

The 14th Key Law

Know when to say no.

Realizing when to say no before its too late is a key factor in winning this game of life. How many times have you said yes and regretted your decision? You cannot tell yourself no while telling someone else yes. Honor the fourteenth Key Law.

21

Cycle 3

Visualization

This is by far the most powerful tool that our brains have. A definite desire cannot be truly definite without visualization. There are many methods of effective visualization. In this chapter we will go over a few ways to make the visualization process more effective for you.

The 15th Key Law

Random thoughts are never random. Write them down.

Have you ever just had a completely irrelevant thought come to mind? Like a thought that has nothing to do with the present moment. Well, this is your intuition working harmoniously with your inner God. We should never ignore a bright idea. You should keep a journal just for random thoughts. Write

them down along with the date. Allow your mind to unfold.

The 16ᵗʰ Key

Always have an out of reach goal to ensure that you're always aiming highly.

No matter where you are in life today, I guarantee that you have seen yourself here before arriving. It is inevitable that you shall arrive at your next destination in life in the very same manner. Why not aim high then? No matter if you feel that you're on

top or at the bottom, there's always room to go up.
Aim high and everything increases.

The 17th Key Law

Industry is virtue.

There is a difference in being in the industry and being the industry. To be in is to follow. This means that you have learned everything from the gains or successes of others. This can be very successful. However, to be the industry is to create a reality that is profound to be the leading example.

The 18th Key Law

Read or write your goals daily.

The old saying "keep your eyes on the prize" speaks volumes with the frequency of the 18th Key Law. Reading and writing are the best ways to allow repetition to create a new reality for the subconscious mind. This key was inspired by the late and great Bob Proctor. He suggests that we write down a powerful affirmation 100 times daily. Try it with your current top goal.

The 19th Key Law

Failing is learning and quitting is quitting.

100 failures equal 99 visions to try again from the very first failure. Definite determination is guaranteed to eventually pay off. One must never quit nor consider the thought as it was never a part of the original visualized plan. Remain focused on success as the plan unravels in your mind. Besides, quitting is a definite loss.

The 20th Key Law

Always visualize debt as a blessing.

Is your glass half empty or half full? How could the frequency of leverage(debt) be anything less than a blessing? For starters, whomever you owe trusts you and your ventures enough to allow you to owe in the first place. Debt is only bad when it's misused, and

you have nothing left to show but the bill. Utilize debt
to get and remain ahead.

The 21ˢᵗ Key Law

Believe in yourself.

What you believe is what you think. What you think is what you become. What you become is what you believe. This cycle is perfect to close out the 3ʳᵈ cycle. Your mind is a computer. Be smart about the thoughts that you download to your hard drive. Don't get hacked by negative thoughts.

33

Cycle 4

Will Power

To be successful in life, you must be willing to use your will power over your memory. Not just the bad memories, but the good ones as well. For example, when I was a kid, my mom used to get off from work and relax for a few hours. Dinner was the only thing she did after work. Most of us do the same thing today waiting on a miracle to save our lives. The miracle is when you realize time is not forever. Down time is the time to work on self to be who you want to be in this life. It just takes a lot of will power.

The 22nd Key Law

Stay out of your head and remain in your body.

It doesn't matter what kind of car you drive or if you
have one at all. Your body is your most important
vehicle. It will take you to every destination that life
has in store for you. To be "in your head" is to be idle.
We all know that idle does not move. Its time to let
go of all your doubts, fears, resentment, and sadness,
as it is time to live.

The 23rd Key Law

Always consider discipline before freedom.

To piggyback on the intro to this cycle, as adults we are free to do as we please. This, however, can be very toxic and is to some. Discipline and freedom are both habits. To be lost in freedom usually means that you have a lot of bad habits that need analyzing. To be disciplined can set you free from bad habits. It will also free your time to make time to be free. Start

**with a daily schedule and go from there. Consistency
is key. Are you disciplined or are you free?**

The 24th Key Law

Don't let your memory be your guide.

You must learn to allow pure willingness to be your intuitive guide in life. Memory is the complete opposite. Be willing to remember the bright future before the bright or dark past events. They do not matter in this present moment. We must all practice remaining in the present moment. We first must be willing to do so.

The 25th Key Law

Stand still and remain calm.

In business and in every other aspect of life, we will face challenging times. It is only inevitable. How we react in these stressful times is the bigger picture of the stressful time. You must be both fair and balanced in all communication. Being upset and/or irate will not change what has already happened to initiate those emotions. Preserve your energy for the brighter days.

The 26th Key Law

Commit to the schedule.

To commit to the schedule, you first need to have one. Being organized is a very high key to success. It will help to free up time that you don't realize you have. Are you willing to commit to the schedule? Scheduling life puts your energy in harmony with the frequency of abundance.

The 27th Key Law

Keep going.

If you don't keep going then you will be where you are today, forever. Set yourself free from this spell. Again, quitting is quitting. Life is momentum with a deadline. The scary part is that nobody knows their deadline. We all have things to get done both now and later. There's no time to waste time.

The 28th Key Law

Protect the brand.

Protecting your brand is like protecting your life. By any means, the show must go on! You cannot take everyone with you along this journey to success. Honor your brand like your own name with personal integrity and pure ambition to thrive. Success is guaranteed if you protect the brand. This is the 28th Key Law.

Cycle 5
Structure

Structure is simply the quality of being organized. Simple but not always easy. Consistency is the key here as you will have to tell yourself no sometimes in order to follow your structural guidelines. Structure is the basis and also the regulated guidelines of your business.

The 29th Key Law

Schedule everything.
Even the routine items.

Writing is a powerful tool to utilize with organizational skills. Scheduling daily tasks is writing out your definite purpose for the universe. You can also see your free time in addition to seeing the time being wasted.

The 30th Key Law

Always seek the good before the bad.

Practicing optimism over pessimism must be the only option. To look for the good is to want the good. This is why my glass will always be half full and never half empty.

45

The 31ˢᵗ Key Law

Be the hardest working individual that you know.

In order to become the hardest working individual that you know, you must surround yourself with others that currently work harder than you. You will pick up and eliminate traits from them all until you reach your personal point of mastery. Now you can create a

schedule that allows you to be the hardest
working individual that you know.

The 32nd Key Law

Build a mastermind alliance with ones that are gifted in your weakest areas.

The power of the mind is priceless. However, the power of multiple minds in harmony with

the same frequency is a guaranteed success. You must first identify without a doubt your true strengths and your true weaknesses. Then match your alliance with the opposites of your strengths and weaknesses. This is now your mastermind alliance.

The 33rd Key
Law

Never waste time.

Time will never end for the universe. However, it is the one guarantee to bet on that time lasts for no one forever. The clock is forever ticking.

The 34th Key Law

Deliver what you promise.

Your word is truly all you have. Opportunities don't come daily for most so keeping your word will solidify your integrity with others. Integrity will get you a long way when you're dependent on people to make your business successful. A loyal client must first trust their patrons with their trust.

The 35ᵗʰ Key Law

Lead from the front.

This is something that I learned for a mentor that was also my bosses boss at the time. I was an assistant manager in a very popular warehouse and I was equal age or younger than the majority of my subordinates. This made it interesting to say the least. My bosses boss always reminded me to simply lead from the front and everything would be fine. I was very good at the actual job that I had become a manager in. With that I showed my team that I

could out-perform most of them and that
definitely earned my respect. Show them why
you are the leader.

Cycle 6
Finance

This is where a lot of discipline is also very necessary. Finance is where it starts and also where it ends. Finances have to be in order to run a successful business. Understanding finances is also important.

The 36th Key Law

Never buy one if you cannot afford ten.

Smart investments are carefully strategized before the light turns green. It's not worth the time if you're investing an amount that you'll only need by next Tuesday. Make sure the cushion is soft before you say green light on any kind of investments.

The 37th Key Law

No matter the amount, keep a consistent savings system going.

How much has the past you done for the present you? Could the present you do more for the future you than the past you did for you now? The time is now to buckle down and start saving. This is essential for the future you and also the perfect setup for future opportunities.

The 38th Key Law

Set your price and stand firm on it.

Never give in and never ever give up. The universe will only react if you have made your definite decision to coincide with your definite purpose. It may seem rough in the beginning but standing firm builds your future better than giving in.

The 39ᵗʰ Key Law

Capital is key.

Would you rather fall on a hard surface or a soft cushion? Well capital is definitely that soft cushion. New businesses need self-assurance so that if anything goes wrong it doesn't become and automatic failure. Capital is the safe net and is needed more than anything when starting a new venture.

The 40th Key Law

Donate regularly.

Sharing is caring and in the business word sharing is solidifying present and future successes. Anything you put into this universe will always come back to revisit you. Why not only put out great blessings?

The 41st Key Law

Never over or under-spend.

Every investment is nothing more than a bet. Though some bets are guaranteed wins, others are not so for sure. This is why before moving into any financial decisions you must first have a plan. This will ensure you can truly HODL and not be a victim of feeling FOMO as they say in the stock and crypto market worlds. A solid

plan will also ensure that you never over or under-spend.

The 42nd Key Law

Only invest in what you can afford to lose.

This is a definite piggyback on the 39th and 41st Key Laws. Accepting the fact of failure will make your definite decisions even more powerful. Though we always plan to win, sometimes the unexpected can throw us off track a bit. You must be prepared for the "what if" factor.

Cycle 7
Self

From the start to the finish of any venture in life, the one denominator that will make or break you is yourself. Are you allowing your self to blossom or are you blocking yourself from blossoming? Are you leading your way or are you in your way? Think about these two questions as we go through the final cycle; Self.

The 43rd Key Law

Remain curious and never judge.

Although curiosity kills cats, it makes some humans filthy rich! To judge is to block your blessings. You won't understand everything in your journey but if you accept that fact then you'll never block a blessing. Someone you may not understand at first could become a power

player in your mastermind alliance if the shoe
fits. Be optimistic always.

The 44th Key Law

Keep 50% of your thoughts to yourself.

We must not distract others with 100% of our thoughts. On the contrary, we must protect our thoughts and ideas from the opinions of others to remain firm in the mindset in place for the task or event. Limited thoughts are often passed out from friends and family. Protect your ears and theirs as well.

The 45ᵗʰ Key Law

Take care of your people.

When running a business, your people are both your associates as well as your clients. It's safe to say that your people are collectively your entire business. To take care of your people is to take care of your business. Listen to them, right or wrong. Hear them out. The

**loyalty from your people will dictate the
longevity of your business.**

The 46ᵗʰ Key Law

Handle every situation with grace.

Your energy is the equivalent to a boomerang. Whatever you put out into this universe is almost guaranteed to come back to revisit you. If grace is all you deliver than grace will be the only thing that you'll receive. Amazing Grace it is. Have some if you don't already.

The 47ᵗʰ Key Law

Remain loyal to your heart.

Intuition is instilled into all of us. Weather we use it or not is the thing. You cannot tell yourself no while telling others yes. The first answer to come to mind is like a hunch and is almost always the right answer. Follow your heart. When it speaks, listen.

The 48th Key Law

Respect is earned.

Self-respect is the key to all aspects of respect. If there is a lack of self-respect then respecting anything will be quite a task. Respect will get you anything that you desire in life. However, it never comes for free.

The 49th Key Law

Always practice perfect self-expression.

Every one of the Key Laws of life has one common denominator, which is your self-expression. The entire book is a complete practice of self-expression. How you present yourself to the world is how you will be perceived. Make it count with every word, jester, and emotion with an out-word signal.

Made in the USA
Columbia, SC
15 October 2022

69379495R00043